Divine
Expressions

BY CARDARIUS K. GRADY

DIVINE EXPRESSIONS!

ISBN 978-0-9853371-1-7

Copyright 2014

Published by

Cardarius K. Gardy

cardariusgrady@yahoo.com

Contents

Acknowledgement

I owe a great many thanks to a great many of people who helped and supported me during the writing of this book.

My deepest thanks go out to Ms. Jean Bloom, LaDarius Felder and Dr. Tenecia Bullock for carefully guiding this project and correcting various documents of mine when it was needed. I also want to thank my personal marketing team for taking the time to support and post many quotes and sayings that I've written throughout the time I was writing the book. The list includes: Darrell Coleman, Shelton Brumfield, Brittany Minor, Delquana Brumfield, Chris Carr, Sequitta Bullock, Dajaun Lipscomb Jacquelyn Hill, Tikia Croom, LaDeania Campbell, and Antalia Collins. I express my thanks to the many teachers at South Pike School District and the Pike County area for their constant support.

Last but not least, I want to extend a great sense of gratitude to my family: Jessie Grady (Mother), Demetris Jackson, and Liketha Armstrong, Briunna Grady (Sisters), Terry and Runner Grady (Brothers), Pastor Kenneth R. Handy and Sister Pasty Handy for their constant love and support throughout this process.

Introduction

Behind the white paint that he wear, is a face that God has created.

The way he move express his true feelings that lives deep within.

Inside his head is a brain with thoughts that no one can phantom.

So he writes to release those thoughts he feels need to be spoken.

Underneath his chest is a heart that has been torn

So he expresses his hurt and pain through a mask that is worn.

Around his eyes lives water that sometimes flow like a river.

So he pen poems and letters to paint a dynamic picture.

On both sides of his face, are ears that capture many different sounds.

So he dance to the rhyme of the beat by moving his feet around and around.

In his writing and dancing are many lessons

So he named them

~ Divine Expressions~

Special Someone

To someone who is as special as you,

Who is faithful and true?

Who know what it takes to make it through,

To someone who is as special as you.

Who still can laugh when times get tough?

Even when the road seems rough,

And you made it through,

To someone who is as special as you.

Who tells the truth when times are blue,

Who helps make dreams come true?

To someone who is as special as you.

Who is amazing in everything that she do,

Who is always encouraging others too?

Who prays until she sees a breakthrough?

Who works when she really don't have to

To someone who is as special as you.

Who loves neighborhood kids as her own?

Who doesn't mind sharing the things in her home?

Who doesn't mind picking up the phone,

And correcting things that are wrong,

Who understands there is nothing new?

To someone who is as special as you.

Whose hope is in God for a better tomorrow?

Whose wisdom is so easy to follow?

Who understand The Bible brings no sorrow,

To someone who is as special as you.

I wrote this story about someone who

is dear and kind and loving too.

So the whole world could see,

Her love and faithfulness is so true,

To that special someone and that's you.

Whatcha Say Now!

When they said I wouldn't amount to anything,
I proved them wrong.
When they said I was no good,
I took out the time and found the good.
When they said I was going to spend the rest of my life in jail,
I pass by it every day praising God because I'm not living in a cell.
When they said I was going to die young,
I'm still living, healthy, and strong.
When they said I couldn't make it without them,
I wonder why they are gone.
When they said I wasn't going to change,
I stand before you today saved, sanctified, and Holy Ghost filled
man.
When they said I was going to be a bomb,
I graduated from college twice and have a good life.
When they said I wasn't called,
Well, why am I still preaching after a great big down fall?
When I was least likely to succeed in high school,
Now, I'm writing books talking about all the things I have
achieved.
When I was looked down on because I grew up poor,
Now, I'm living a life of true happiness and joy.
When they look at me with the expressions Wow!!!!
I respond by saying Whatcha Say Now!!!

Caught in the Cross Fire

Caught between two is normally how it happen,

When one does not have the knowledge to complete a task, the other one is called on to satisfy that fleshly desire.

Playing with people feeling is the reason why relationships, marriages, and friendships fall because you cannot treat those people that God placed in your life any kind of way and think its ok.

Being dragged along and treated like a segment floating in a half empty glass by the one you though loved you is such a hurtful feeling because after what's done in the dark comes to the light the mind being to wonder and the fight begin,

The fight mentally, emotionally, socially, and physically is normally the result because when someone tries to have their cake and eat it too it causes hurt and pain to others.

People come and people go but trying to hold on to two because one out does the other one in a certain area is a selfish and childish mindset.

However, when going through these times, you must remember that those who part took in this wrong will receive their prosper punishment because God will not allow anyone to used and abused without chastening those individuals.

Even though it hurts enormously, it is also a listen learned.

Follow the Yellow Brick Road

L. Frank Baum wrote and released a film called "The Wonderful Wizard of Oz. In this film, a young girl by the name of Dorothy had a dog named Toto who bit her neighbor "Almira Gulch." After Toto bitted Ms. Gulch, Dorothy decided to run away from home for two reasons. The first reason was that her Aunt Em, Uncle Henry, Hunk, Hickory, and Zeke whom she was living with in Kansas did not have time to pay her any attention. (Can you say lonely?) Secondly, she ran away because she wanted to save her dog from being destroyed by Ms Gulch. Upon her running away, she ran across a fortune teller name Professor Marvel who tricked her into believing that her aunt was ill. After hearing that information, Dorothy rushed home to find her home caught up in a tornado. The world wind was so high that it caught her and Toto up and landed them in a Technicolor world of Oz in Munchkin Land.

As she gets herself together, she finds that she was in a place of unknown because there was no familiarity there. Even though she met the Scarecrow, Tin Man, and Cowardly Lion, she still felt alone because they did not know how to lead her back to her homeland. But, it was not until she discovered and decided to Follow the Yellow Brick Road. Some times in our lives we have to be tossed to and fro in order for us to realize that "There is no place like home." Even though home has problems but at least we are around those who have the ability to comfort us and help us in the time of need. Many of us today are in places that we wish we was not in but because things was not going the way we thought they ought to go, we ended up in a place of true isolation and loneliness.

And, while we are out there, the enemy plays with our minds to force us to think no one cares about us but it is until we realize that home is the place to be. Because at home, we can find true love, joy, peace, happiness, family, and friends. So, if you are that person who is in that place, I encourage you to Follow the Yellow Brick Road because it will lead you back home.

Just a Form of Mist

As I sit out in the ocean and stare at the mist, somehow a beautiful face appears.

A face that one time did not exist.

A face that amazes me because it's a face I can plainly see.

A face that lit up my night.

So I'm wondering am I seeing this right.

So as I roll my boat closer to see, disappointment strikes me heavy.

As I approach, the clouds start too swift

Then I realize that face "Was Just a Form of Mist."

Do you know love?

If we really knew what love meant, the world would be a better place because there would be true peace, and we would want for others what we wanted for ourselves.

If we really knew what love meant, we wouldn't mind our neighbor correcting our child because we would know they had the same spirit as we, and the correcting was done out of love.

If we really knew what love meant, divorce rates wouldn't be so high because couples believed in their vows and considered them worth fighting for.

If we really knew what love meant, churches would stop fighting over denominations and just serve God in spirit and in truth, and the world would see and live the embodiment of God's love on a daily basis in their lives.

If we really knew what love meant, mothers would accept their daughters back after they went out and had a baby before marriage with the love and compassion that God has shown them.

If we really knew what love meant, fathers would make sure their sons have the right teaching, so when they grow up they would know the strengths, compassion, and courage that makes a true man of God.

If we really knew what love meant, we would feed the homeless because we are all one family in Christ; and we take care of our family.

And if we really knew what love meant, we would love each other through the good and the bad because we are always conscious of God's love for us which always calls us to pass it on.

If we only knew what love really meant.

The 1st Lady

The first lady is like none other because now she's everybody mother,

The first lady lives, talks, prays, and teaches others secrets that will help them go further.

The first lady is also the backbone to her husband,

The first lady covers him while he is away because she knows people will try to throw darts in his face.

The first lady stays up with her husband when he's feeling down;

The first lady comforts him when no one else is around.

The first lady supports her husband when times get hard.

The first lady knows she is his angel and his personal bodyguard.

The first lady gives her all because she knows that one day the ministry will spread abroad.

The first lady is very unique,

Because she doesn't believe in defeat,

Plus she likes everything neat.

The first lady takes care of her home.

The first lady understands sometimes things may go wrong;

The first lady is one you can depend on.

The first lady never quits,

Because she knows God is going to bring her through all of this.

Step Follow

In June 15, 1995, Disney released a movie called "The Lion King". In this particular movie, I discovered that sometimes it seems like we have made the wrong choice or have moved to wrong place. But, even when it seems like we are in the wrong place because of the decisions we have had, we are actually in the place where God want us to be. We have to understand that sometimes God have to allow some uncontrollable things to happen in our lives so He can develop us.

For example, Simba did not have the power to control what happen to him in his past or the choice he had to make in leaving his home land. But isn't it amazing how things turn right back around for him? Because when his true destiny called his name, he couldn't fight it. He had to Step Follow and handle his responsibility because his development stage was over. I said that to say this. I know the situation might not look good for you right now but remember God is preparing you to walk into your destiny. So, press through the wilderness because things are going to turn around for you. And when true destiny calls your name Step Follow because There Is King in You!!

You are not alone

The pain that's hidden with a smile.
The heart that's hidden but really needs fixing.
The soul that steady cries out, yearning for someone's ears to
listen;
The nights of not sleeping the days of not eating
Sorrow has come and taken the life that was once in you
Pain stole your joy.
Hurt wounded your spirit.
Thinking of all your troubles and all who have killed the love
you had,
You throw in the towel; you quit; you say to yourself I'm
tired of all of this.
Jesus hears & he sees.
His love is like a warm embrace upon you when you bow on
your knees.
He softly speaks to you, "Live" You shall live and not die.
Trust God!
Give your pain, your hurt to Jesus and watch him move in
your life.
He will turn your life around; He'll restore your joy, your
brokenness.
You are not alone.
Jesus is with you.

The Church

The church is the place where God's Glory is reveal;

It's the place where people come to be healed.

The church is the place where people come to get taught,

It's the place where Jesus finds no fault,

The church is the place where lives are transforming,

It's the place where hurting people are coming,

The church is the place where we worship and praise God,

It's the place where we give Him our all,

The church is the place where everyone is invited,

It's the place where the saints are excited,

The church is the place where true love is shown,

It's the place where some people came home,

The church is the place where everyone is free,

It's the place where people can lay at Jesus' feet,

The church is the place where everyone plays apart,

It's a place where you don't have to be smart,

The church is the place to gain strength for tomorrow,

It's the place where you can always go to the altar,

The church is the place where people pray,

It's the place where souls are saved,

The church is the place we are taught great lesson,

It's the place where we prepare ourselves to enter heaven.

A True Friend

A True Friend tells the truth,
Even when it hurts you,
A True Friend encourages you,
When everyone else put you down.
A True Friend watches your back,
In front of your enemy.
A True Friend makes you smile
When you want to frown,
A True Friend gives you their all,
Even when you fall,
A True Friend loves,
Even in the midst of a flood,
A True Friend knows exactly what to say,
When you have been betrayed,
A True Friend is always near,
When you need a listening ear,
A True Friend sends you a breeze,
When you are in fear,
A True Friend will stay,
When things don't go their way,
A True Friend will do all they can do
Even when they don't have a clue
Of the things you're really going through,
I believe that's a true friend.
What about you?

Built to Last

A few ago, Chevrolet came out with a commercial and in the commercial they inserted a song called "Like A Rock" by Bob Seger. After doing some research, I discovered that the company inserted that song to inform the world that this new vehicle they were advertising was built to outlast any stormy weather. Not only are those features like none other. Chevrolet realize if they were able to convince the word that it will never find any other vehicle like this one they would make a huge amount on sales. In order words, if a man can build a vehicle that is able to withstand the potholes in the road, rain, sleet, and snow, what you think God did when He created us?

Special Place

There is a special place in you,

Where extraordinary power lies,

There is a special place in you

Where hope and courage has not died.

There is a special place in you,

Where your spirit cries,

There is a special place in you,

Where broken pieces want to be revised,

There is a special place in you

Where faith has to be applied,

There is a special place in you,

Where God's Word must rise,

There is a special place in you,

That has been overlooked and denied.

There is a special place in you,

That needs to be brought back alive.

The Gift

Over two thousand years ago, there was a gift given to the world.

The gift that was born by way of a virgin girl.

Over two thousand years ago, there was a gift given to the world.

The gift that God wanted to share.

Over two thousand years ago, there was a gift given to the world.

The gift that really cares.

Over two thousand years ago, there was a gift given to the world.

The gift that judges everyone fair.

Over two thousand years ago, there was a gift given to the world.

The gift that can repair.

Over two thousand years ago, there was a gift given to the world.

The gift that is rare.

Over two thousand years ago, there was a gift given to the world.

The gift that walked on air.

Over two thousand year ago, there was a gift given to the world.

The gift that always stayed in prayer.

Over two thousand years ago, there was a gift given to the world.

The gift that that God shared to His people in despair.

Live Without

Can you imagine a river flowing without the stream?

Can you imagine grass growing without turning green?

Can you imagine waves boasting without the eastern
wind?

Can you imagine stars shining bright throughout the
night?

Can you imagine clouds riding smooth without the
prosper sun light?

Can you imagine true love flowing without a pure heart?

Can you imagine a tree living without its roots?

Can you imagine a honeycomb that does not attract bees?

Can you imagine living your life without me?

Believe In Yourself

A few years ago, I decided to go on a quest to find the answer to success. After trying different things and failing, I discovered the answer I was looking for was in a small book that was published in 1930 in the United States called "The Little Engine that Could." After carefully reading the book, I realize that no matter how hard things may get if we keep working hard we can do it. In the book, Watty Piper used something simple as a small blue train to convey a positive message to his readers. The illustration of the train trying to pull a huge cargo over a steep hill was a way to let us know that if we trust and believe in ourselves we can do the impossible.

Many times we allow what we see to throw us off course because what we see causes us to feel a certain way. But, if we could just dig deep within ourselves and tap into that inner power that was placed in us when we were born, we can climb any mountain. Not only that, but if we spend time developing our minds and look at every situation as an opportunity to succeed eventually it will happen. According to Dictionary.com, believe mean to have faith and confidence in. In other words, if we do not have faith in ourselves who will? One thing I discovered about the little blue train is when the task got hard it went for help. Even though many of the bigger trains turned her down, she never gave up because she knew that if she kept trying soon or later she was going to achieve her goal.

So, I encourage you to believe in yourself because once you do that God will do the rest

I Do

Today as I take your hand,

And as I follow God's plan,

A new life we shall began,

With true happiness and love flowing.

Today as I take your hand,

I vow to be your husband,

And provide for the house so our lives can advance,

With true worship and praise to God,

I believe we can.

Develop a great and awesome master plan.

Today as I take your hand,

I vow to love and cherish you.

Always listen to God to bring us through

Today it's me and you,

God, Jesus, and The Holy Ghost too,

So this is point where I say I do.

Praise Break

I can't forget what He's done for me,

Way back on Calvary.

When I think about His Story,

I have to give Him Glory.

He suffered and hung on a tree,

Just to set me free.

He didn't have to do it, but He did,

So, I believe, He deserves more then I can give

Because when I look back over my life, I can say He's real,

So, sitting by me might have been a mistake,

Because I don't know how long it's going to take

For me to finish

This Praise Break

Visualize

Can you visualize yourself in the place you have never been before?

The place where you always dreamed of,

Living the life that you only see on the television show,

The life that many people spend their whole life working for;

The place where you don't have to worry anymore,

The place where you spent time preparing for,

And the place where true love is not abhorred,

The place where it's now easy to enjoy,

The place where the water is crystal clear like on the Island Timor;

The place where that does exist but only so far,

The place that sits beyond the shore,

The place where the mansion has many golden floors;

And the place where there is no war.

The place where you only want more.

The Pastor's Struggle

He often struggles with his destiny because no one understands his call,

He stays awake day and night listening to God so the church won't fall,

He spends his time visiting nursing homes and hospitals,

He tutors at the schools,

He feeds families,

He evangelizes,

He mentors,

He provides and protects his family,

He studies first, to live, then, preach and teach God's Word,

So the people can establish a closer relationship with Him,

He wants everyone to be blessed,

So he serves the community with passion and zeal,

So God's Glory can be revealed,

On the other hand, he also deals with the enemy attacking his character,

Placing people in his atmosphere to be unsupportive,

To Backbite,

To Gossip,

And to slander his name,

But he knows, through all the heartaches and pain,

God sees his faithfulness and is going to reward him according to his works.

A Special Tribute

The time that we shared was short but fun;

No one understood why we were talking and texting all day on the phone.

We share many secrets about our lives and the things we have done,

Like when you shot grandma's dog with pawpaw's nail gun.

There are so many things that I remember,

Like the times you went off on one of the church members.

It's like we were two of a kind

Until death rolled up, took you, and left me behind

To deal with all the memories that's running through my mind,

Like when you broke that old woman in the grocery line.

Man, how I miss those times,

But I know you had to go;

So, I wrote this to let the world know.

That even though you're not here

Your life will always run through the minds of those far and near

To remind us not to fear,

Because God is going wipe away every tear!

No One Knows

No one knows the pain I feel,

No one see the river of tears,

No one understand the love that follows through my heart,

No one understand how it feel to be set apart,

No one knows how bad I've been broken,

No one knows how I almost gave up hoping,

No one feel my pain of rejection,

No one knows how to show real affection,

No one knows how hard I work to make my dream come true,

No one is there when I need them to

And no one is there willing to lend a helping hand,

That's why the Bible say depend on God and not man

Ready or Not

Will you be ready when Jesus returns?

Or will you be still playing games?

Will you be ready to change in a twinkling of an eye?

Or will your attitude towards God remain the same?

Will you be ready to meet Jesus on high?

Or will you remain on earth preparing to die

Will you be here where when Satan set his kingdom on the earth?

Or will you be looking down at tribulation from the top of the universe?

The day will come that many will not be able to eat,

So prepare yourself for God's victory and Satan's defeat.

Cry

There is a cry that lives inside of me.

There is a cry that no one can see.

There is a cry that is unique.

There is a cry that calls for help.

There is a cry that will make your heart melt.

There is a cry that sings many hurtful songs.

There is a cry for home sweet home.

There is a cry that wants to get out.

There is a cry that keeps water rolling down my sheets.

There is a cry that pushes me to stand on my own two feet.

There is a cry that was caused by hurt and pain.

There is a cry that only God can name.

Untold

There is a story about a beautiful rose that has not been exposed.

Because this beautiful rose has some experiences that no one knows.

There is a story about a beautiful rose who self-esteem was once froze.

Because this beautiful rose was once hurt and left out in the cold.

There is a story about a beautiful rose that once up tight and hard to unfold.

Because this beautiful rose had not recovered from its last love episode.

There is a story about a beautiful rose that love runs deep but is afraid to let go.

Because this beautiful rose cannot keep her emotions under control.

There is a story about a beautiful rose that cries so much.

 Because she has not found an answer to the question that lives deep within her soul.

There is a story about a beautiful rose who have tried to live beyond the mold.

But, she can't because her story will remain untold.

What Should I Do

Where do I begin?

What should I say?

To this woman that has taken my breath away.

How do I tell her?

To let her know that she has made my day.

Where do I go?

Who can I talk to?

To paint a picture of the beauty that has passed this way.

Should I go after her?

Or should I stay in amaze?

Well, I think I'm following that face.

Wait!!!

How do I approach her?

In what fashion and what way?

Because I can't even articulate the right words to say.

I Am A Man

I am a man with Purpose.
I am a man with Character.
I am a man with Power.
I am a man with Integrity.
I am a man with Respect.
I am a man that demands Respect.
I am a man with Zeal.
I am a man that Gives.
I am a man with Love.
I am a man with Knowledge.
I am a man with Pride.
I am a man with Style.
I am a man with Confidence
I am a man with Courage.
I am a man with Determination.
I am a man with Expectations
I am a man of Valor
I am a man of Virtue.
I am a man of Honesty.
I am a man of Humility.
I am a man of Harmony.
I am a man of Enthusiasm.
I am a man of Persistence.
I am a man of Vision.
I am a man of Faith.
I am a man of Prayer.
Most of all, I am a man of God.

The Letter From My Father

Before you were born, I knew what you were going to be. When you were born, I gave you back to God because I had no idea how I was to supposed to raise someone special, like you. Many nights I walked by your room and cried because I was happy that God trusted me with you. You changed my life in many different ways. You pushed me to do the impossible because I wanted to be the best father a son could have. I have made many mistakes as a man and most of all as your father. If I knew what I know now, I would have instructed you better because I wanted the best for you, but I see there were some things only God could teach you. I watched you grow from a boy to a man and developed a great and awesome plan. You taught me the meaning of fatherhood, and I am thankful for your presence. There were many things I wanted to tell you, but time ran short, so as I pen this letter, I want you to know that I love you and wish you well. My son this life is hard, and it can send you on a roller coaster if you allow it to, on the other hand, life can be fun if you make the best of it. As long as you live, remember there are a lot of things you are going to face in this life and in your ministry that is going to cause you a lot of hurt and pain. You are going to make many mistakes just as I've done, and everyone is not going to like you, but if you stay faithful, God will bring you through it. You were chosen by God before the foundation of the world to be a spokesman for Him. I am proud of you, Son, for not neglecting the gift and the call. Now that I am gone remember to stand for what is right, provide for your family, invent something new, write a book, but most of all Preached the Word!!!

In Loving Memory of Runner Grady Sr.

www.ingramcontent.com/pod-product-compliance
Lightning Source LLC
Chambersburg PA
CBHW060634030426
42337CB00018B/3350